WHERE THE SIDEWALKS MEET

"This is a view of the inside of the other side of the America that's seldom seen with such bravado and honesty in American poetry—an immigrant Black and Brown America ripped open by White rage and indifference. Recinos's view of the role Christianity plays in all this is equally profound and original. These are poems that needed to be written—truthful, often-enraged poems written by and for the soul."

—PHILIP SCHULTZ,
author of The God of Loneliness

"Written with immeasurable grit and grace. Recinos is an unfeigned apostle for minor voices. . . . With a gentle ambush motivating every poem, *Where the Sidewalks Meet* is an unabridged testament for how to listen, sense, feel, experience those who get 'used to the world looking at [them] sideways'; for in Recinos's stunning stanzas, every line is an imperative, an intention for a more honorable universe."

—SANDRA RUIZ,
author of Ricanness

"In *Where the Sidewalks Meet*, a poetic consciousness roams New York, creating a cartography of the inner-city experience. These poems exist at the crossroad of life, history, and consciousness. Fast-paced as urban life it-self, these verses demand to be read aloud, sometimes like a vignette evoking childhood, sometimes like a diary, sometimes as a statement of values, sometimes as a cry for help and social justice, sometimes as a prayer for the fallen, but always as living poetry."

—CARLOS AGUASACO,
author of The New York City Subway Poems

"Compassion swings the lines here in this poetry of openhearted vision . . . . 'Sweet words' witness life on the margins of the American myth. We can see the stars right alongside the scars, the spangles right next to the anguish, and the angels in the Spanglish informing these propulsive prayers, which sometimes turn from grief to glory and back in a single well-turned phrase. A beautiful, layered, heartful reading experience."

—MARIA DAMON,
author of Postliterary America

"*Where the Sidewalks Meet* is a robust book that calls out and combats the wickedness of a national imagination that would dispossess its people. . . . Recinos leans into poetry's direct power to (re)name the forces threatening our shared humanity—ignorance, bigotry, fear—and the effect is a resonance that reckons with the risk, an intensity that tries to 'restart [the] heart,' poems that hold if not yoke us across a country of difference."

—GEFFREY DAVIS,
author of Night Angler

WHERE THE SIDEWALKS MEET

Harold J. Recinos

RESOURCE *Publications* • Eugene, Oregon

WHERE THE SIDEWALKS MEET

Resource Publications
An Imprint of Wipf and Stock Publishers
199 W. 8th Ave., Suite 3
Eugene, OR 97401

www.wipfandstock.com

PAPERBACK ISBN: 978-1-6667-3146-0
HARDCOVER ISBN: 978-1-6667-2398-4
EBOOK ISBN: 978-1-6667-2400-4

DECEMBER 6, 2021 9:43 AM

CONTENTS

PERFECT

brown child knocking on the
door, turning away from the
deaf world, shedding tears for
cruel old men who never stretch
a hand to dark skin and look down
at your tender face, I will open it for
you. scorned little Spanglish girl,
daughter, sister, grandchild of this
prodigious earth, I will open the door
and say you are perfect like heaven
and made with Spanglish bricks found
on South Bronx rubble lots.

THE PLAGUE

the toddlers from San Salvador
who were locked up in jails, sent
home in a cheap box when they
stopped breathing and lost in the
system for more than a year remind
me of Oscar Romero killed by an
American paid for sharp shooter at
the altar in the church. how long will
America go on killing Saints and taking
the life of the innocent? How long will
the good English-speaking churches keep
on sitting on the pews upholstered with
our skin in silence?

PURGATORY

we heard it said here
the crooked who have
lived in this country
reducing dark skinned
humanity to ashes seem
to go straight. well, we
think time has never been
riper to say Dante's seven
terraces of sin called pride,
envy, wrath, sloth, avarice,
gluttony, and lust made on
earth by imperial white might
dashed the hope of heaven
on earth and won a bitterly
warm purgatorial stay. you see,
we crossed the desert just last
week talking that God's Mariachi
band is singing in purgatory America
hurry and plead your white depravities
for the mercy plan. what will happen
to the people who have defined the
stomping ground with the broken flesh
of Black humanity, asylum seeking
Latinas' with kids and dances around
the lynching trees? will white lunatics

3

purge their wicked souls and find the
stairs that lead to heaven's door? we
floated across the Rio Grande talking
in soft Spanish perhaps these Gringos
will not be pardoned after leaving the
smell of rotting bodies on earth and
breaking every message that came
from above. you see, nothing can be
kept hidden in purgative space where
our tear-stained brown checks and your
snowy white faces see each other. listen,
we can tell you in the broken English you
detest that evil here is out of reach, heaven
is nearly visible and it may be time for you
to ask how long until a pale faced soul gets
paroled to the Nazarene's gran fiesta? perhaps,
a fresh good book will push up out of the ground
and with so much time on our scabbed souls, we
will get a chance to read it and give the great
yonder another look.

HELL

observe the road with flames
along its edges that crackle
with limbs while faces line the
way with agonized expressions.
have a look at the perverted users
of language, the money grubbing
assholes of alternative reality,
the soiled orange lovers of cruelty,
murder, torture, petrified bullshit
and pimply wickedness. open your
eyes wide to take a good look at the
cunning slum lords, foul-mouthed
preachers, fetid politicians, racists
dogmatists and the parade of white
supremacist obstructors of truth now
genuinely at home. recall sitting on
a mound of maggots how Maria said
hell is having tear gas tossed at you
by guards at the border, children ripped
from mothers' arms, toddlers dropping
dead alone in cages in dark American
nights, white cops full of wickedness
squeezing life out of Black men, fitting
brown bodies with holes and cracking
jokes about it all to satisfy the malignant

stupidity of family, supporters and prized

Klan friends. take a deep breath to smell

the burning flesh and remember you were

told hell is Dixieland, the barrio, the toxic

fields, worksites, cities, churches, schools

and places devils run free on earth to sicken

blameless souls. hell may even be too kind

to you giving you an eternity to realize the

party is over and those who armed themselves

against injustice are dancing Salsa in heaven

with Tito Puente, Celia Cruz and all the other

good people in life you despised and shamelessly

bled or hung from trees.

PARADISO

it happened kicking cans down
a littered street, when heaven it
seemed made it to the slum. hope
passed over us like the wind and
the One drenching the block with
light shined for a time on the widows,
undocumented kids, single young
mothers, just paroled teens, junkie
old men, aging street walkers and
Tony the Spanish speaking cop to
let them feel a brief moment of peace
and get a glimpse of God in the alley
spray painting a message on Lefty's
building that said I the maker of all
things am always with you. the sacred
truths the people sing point the way to
paradise, where crushed *Spics* like me
whisper Spanglish prayers sounding like
lost lines of sublime verse Angels must
carry to heaven's gate where Christ waits
for us to stagger in. travelers on this stony road
wash themselves in the salty waters of Orchard
Beach where beauty from battered bodies rises
and sandy children at play find ways to explain
paradise has a different address, no ticking clocks,

no white people demanding you speak English
and the world there together ends. on this earth
so full of people with little grace the wretched
of the earth who perennially bear witness to stones
that speak declare today in paradise we will
live without church bells ringing, mothers
howling above graves, people with souls
packed with pain, politicians robed with
doom, and cops beating and killing us in
their white history or worry about God not
willing to bend to hear us cursing the blood
that dripped from the Cross that never was
enough to save. yes, paradise will be found
easily by the brokenhearted and peace will
squeeze through the cracks of the bloody
organ after allowing us a brief peak at the
first and absolute reality some have flattered
with major and minor names.

LONG WALK

we walked in donated shoes
for miles praying on the road
without waiting for answers,
occasionally stopping in the
shade to kneel in the open air
like the last time in the church
where God spoke Spanish and
busses passed in front of it filling
us with fumes. we asked to be like
the wind that blows across borders,
touches every face and speaks the
language of the gate. we walked
some more and again stopped to
hold hands in prayer asking for
God to lift the coffin lid that keeps
us from the free world and rising
from the dead. the walk was something
like a prayer, the sky the vaulted ceiling
of Romero's Cathedral and the shivering
bodies a sign of hope in a very tearful
departure to find a new home. we walked
to the border, the place with a complicated
story, kicking stones on land stolen in the
name of the cross and fearing the people
of the English Book would turn their backs

on us. still, we walked as someone waited

for us!

SANCTUARY

the city flinches at night
with the homeless on the
sidewalks who give no sign
God is nearby. I walk pass
the winos praying for them
to hold in their dirty hands
bread that will let them know
every debt is paid. in the little
park that was once the center
of protests lifting the horrors
of a sinful white nation, I see
junkies adoring temptations in
a world that will bring them to
an end. I cannot see very far in
the dark, but in this city, I know
the people who stumble wearing
thorned hats to make it easier for
the Holy savior to find them. I
look down the street and promise
to do my best to make the darkness
tremble more than the old creaking
pews in the near empty neighborhood
church.

MI BARRIO

nobody on the other side of
town shouts out the names of
barrio kids, knows what to call
the streets where they live nor
ever imagined the disastrous
schools the dark-fleshed barrio
boys and girls attend. nobody
living in the posh condos with
Black and Brown uniformed
doormen has any idea about the
spot on the corner occupied by
tattooed junkies scratching the
scars they carefully plowed on
their arms, legs, hands and feet
as life circled around them not
sure how long it would hang
around. nobody has imagined
what they call the slum is named
home by mothers with dreams who
left villages and towns from different
parts of the Americas or their kids
who speak with Spanglish tongues
that invent almost by the hour new
words of blessing. nobody on the
other side of town can understand
us for claiming life a divine gift,
God undocumented or launching
revolutions and border crossing walks
because of the bendiciones offered by
abuelitas who notice distant lights.

MADRES/MOTHERS

we live each day the life
you gave, hear you whisper
when shadows are long
and experience the touch
of your tender hands in us.
impossible it is to forget the
kisses you gave, the tears
you wiped, the bread you
shared and your dreams
dancing in our veins. today,
we remember the love you
opened in us by which we
see the ebullient beauty of
the world.

THE BEACH

I walked across the little bridge
wearing a pair of fake Converse
sneakers that went well with the
polished linoleum floor in our top
floor apartment but never earned
the right to make a public tour. I
can tell you they were the best hide
shoes available to me from a big old
empty closet with pants in it too short
to argue with God. the sun leaked into
the summer day and there were only
six blocks left to reach the river that
was a little piece of heaven for all
the kids from the block. we spent
long days swimming in the murky
water, imagining the filthy little spot
was a beach on our mothers' Caribbean
island, while acting like a bunch of extras
in West Side Story. I discovered for
the first time the word liberation at the
little creek. you see, we made a beach
front by liberating five huge bags of
sand from a construction site that might
have kept Saint Augustine more morally
besieged than for his Pear theft. yes, the

delinquency was wrong but I can tell you
no one delighted in the act and as good
catholic kids we believed the tiny stumble
that put sand bags in our hands was worth
it just to have a private beach   I confess
exercising the imagination by coming up
with a nice Spanglish name for this little
piece of heaven that belonged to us: Sin
Vergüenza Beach (in public school English
you can take it to mean Shameless Beach)!

PSALM 27

some kids sitting on the stoop
have no fear in the world saying
God is light keeping them unafraid.
these kids never stumble when the
wicked come round the block and
how they laugh when the vile fools
fall. they say you don't even have
to attend church to dwell in the house
of the Lord, since the sky above their
heads and even the bus polluted air
is no less the Lord's dwelling place.
you should hear them shout in the
middle of the night from the building
entrance for the savior to just show
up and take a stand against the people
who look at the barrio discharging
malicious accusations against kids
like them. the whole year long they
wait on a merciful God to offer hope
that is real and they have in their love
for each other learned the good way
quite perfectly on the high steps of
the broken stoop.

COLOR ME CHRIST

I never did see a thorn-crowned
colored Jesus in the Lilly white
church that elevated conquest,
slavery and genocide to a noble
crusade in its book of civilizing
savages in the name of Western
superiority. I have yet to hear a
homily in a big steeple church
that reflects how God made
flesh and populated the world
from darkness with the creative
light that shines brilliantly in the
souls of people in my barrio who
are beaten, tortured and dangled
from trees like Christ. I would
like to hear just once that Jesus
came to this side of the world
darker than snow with good
news to stop violence, dispossession
and denial of self-determination
to people who believed in other
gods and lacked fair skin. I have
waited many years to hear the
simple confession of darn right
shame from my white brothers
and sisters who have embraced
the centuries-long error spread
by theologians and scholars about
the whiteness of God that has not
by any evidence healed a damn thing.
I have thought hard about this point: if
Christ is white and full of lies then with
Langston I must declare move over for
you're getting in the way of people who
will not be sold, stomped and told their

lives in Black, Brown, Yellow and Red
don't matter.

LOST DAYS

on an evening walk I wondered

what happened to the lost days

that manage to give me a little

glimpse of themselves on the

city streets? often, I think of them,

and can even hear my voice crack,

when I stop to sit on a stoop while

the darkness rushes toward the next

day's light. whatever became of the

sketches of tearful clowns I drew for

Mrs. Blankfield in the sixth grade, the

blind kid in the library of the junior high

school with a tutor learning braille, Tito

who loved to ride the subway downtown

just to see what white people were doing

at work, the music teacher from Queens

who played Irish tunes on an accordion

in a four-clover pub, the family clothesline

in the alley where a Jewish violinist played

music unknown to the Puerto Ricans who

tossed change to him that was always wrapped

in newsprint from El Diario La Prensa? I pray

sometimes for the lost days to speak back just

so I can record what they have to say on my

iPhone and keep that sweetness near enough

to upset the angry gods of the country that
plots against us and covers up all the terrible
stories it has written on other lands.

FEEBLE GOD

I could see hackling dogs
in the alley trying to put
their mouths into the same
garbage can that stank of
last night's bones. Angel
in the alley with them was
too poor any day of the week
and at night when he sat with
a bottle of Colt 45 wishing he
could live in the building that
knew him as a little boy. in another
life, Angel would hold a university
post teaching students the world
of the poor, the dreams of Central
America's campesinos and the cries
of the Puerto Rican migration. likely,
he would talk to students about Indians
in the Americas with no childhood,
mothers asking bosses for permission
to bury their kids, soldiers in Guatemala
who shouted long live the Army before
cutting out the tongues of young boys
and gangs annihilating innocence on
bleeding village streets. Angel never
got that call though he is an expert of

many things, the police, the prostitutes,

drunks and junkies on Simpson Street.

I can tell you this with certainty for Angel

was a friend who never stopped demanding

bread even the day he died on a park bench

in the little park on the avenue next to the

old telephone building.

DIRTY FACES

have you seen the little kids
with dirty faces playing on the
streets today, the ones who go
visit a friend at dinner for a plate
of rice, with mothers wrapped
in poverty, regularly slapped by
insults, sexually harassed at work
and abused by men in apartments
that are too dark for light? have
you noticed the angry children
living in cardboard boxes in an
empty slum lot, seen the different
national flags displayed on them,
watched them cry of hunger and
scratching unbathed skin delighting
the fleas that share the space they
call home? their lives were clearly
outlined in the evening news long
before the churches where they so
loudly sing of love whispered how
they deplore these dirty faced kids
with Black and Brown skin. I was
one those kids in your white world
of suspects and life will never be
squeezed out of our colorful dark
souls bubbling over with a divine
simplicity sustained by thousands
of Spanglish words.

THOU SHALT NOT KILL

I am wondering what to say to
you about all the crooked days,
the solutions to the troubles that
are darker than skin, the stumbling
walks bubbling with fear, the weight
of a past full of white hate and a future
God alone knows. I would like to tell
you the branding irons, hanging ropes,
unwelcome words, racist manufactured
destinies and the actions cutting Black
and Brown hearts will not finally reign
supreme in the country that has for so
long been a mound of blindness. I
cannot tell you how long the terrifying
vertigo will last, when they will stop
killing us, the precise time of day the
laws will be fixed and the haunting
white crimes against humanity forced
into the pit of justice. I can only say
that woven into the beautiful texture
of the lives that matter is the surest
tenderness of love that has brought
us all this far even on those days no
one doubted God was too far away
to hear prayers.

THE MASS

I went to a church today with
friends from a family that has
been Catholic since Spanish
was first spoken on this side
of the world. the priest sprinkled
the faithful with baptismal water
to help them recall the beginning
and I swear the faces in the sanctuary
appeared entirely submerged in a
sacred well. I observed elderly women
sitting in their favorite pews with
hands remembering every darling
page in the Holy scriptures and they
even recited the words of traditional
confessions from memory. I prayed
with people never hardened by the
ghostly days of struggle in this English
speaking world, watched dreams with
them dancing on a divine altar cared
for by a Mexican priest who trampled
the naked shadows in the lunatic gardens
of a divided world with a simple homily
of love. I engaged in all the ritual habits
of worship, knelt at length with others to
gaze more deeply at the cross on a wall
behind the Eucharist and was struck by
the feeling this is the place the mystery
of love plays hide and seek with us.

LOS NIÑOS

they dream with big pieces of
chalk in their tiny hands in front
of the brick buildings and sketch
stick figure bodies that dance at the
mercy of the South Bronx wind to
undo the omens lurking in their over
crowded apartments. when these children
look up at the sky crosses from the ancient
world can be seen dangling around their
Brown necks and they seem always to find
so many ways to laugh together in a world
where joy is not forbidden. they look forward
to the mornings that arrive with open eyes,
embrace their self-educated mothers like it
was a time of prayer and then run outside
yelling Spanish words that shock trees in
the little park to grow new leaves and orders
grass to push out from cracks on the gray
sidewalk. their blindness to the world that
finds thousands of ways to despise the color
of their skin, the Holy altars in their homes
and the Spanish they speak has served them
better than bitterness. these children will one
day grow up to get a clear view of the twisted
things they first heard on the foot trails that
delivered them to the city and they will pluck
out thorns from injured flesh by recalling days
of thick innocence in a world thirsty for light
that is not dim.

CAGES

the kids who died
in border cages cried
alone in Spanish to a
deaf country that never
bothered to understand
a single word. the alarm
was not sounded loudly
in the churches, the rich
were busy getting richer
and on the river banks and
aged village streets people
weep.

GLASS JESUS

I visited a church with
carefully placed stained
glass images around the
sanctuary like precious
rocks full of color in a
dark place to catch your
eye. my eyes begged
for clarity when caught
by the image of a white
Jesus looking up in the
Garden of Gethsemane.
the thought occurred to
me this white brother on
the block would be loved
for making water turn into
divine label wine, making
the IRS give back money
to the poor and converting
people who show up at the
church just hating everything
about their dark brothers and
sisters. that morning I could
not keep from thinking this
white Jesus does not reflect
the image at all in which my
dark kin and me were made,
he doesn't know the middle
east, rope neckties, murder on
Central American streets damned
by his white supremacist friends
and the obscene blasphemy of the
segregated hours that come and
go each week while government
officials have the nerve to say teach
the good side of slavery, murder, and

rape. I wondered what the white Jesus prayed for in the Garden, perhaps to keep on making wrong sense in the world with his white brand of old time religion.

AWAKE

no need to rush the waking
hour before the birds soft
whistles. let their songs
gently come and seduce you
into the light of day. count the
seconds gladly for the chariots
may very well swing low to
find you in the next hour like
a favorite gem.

THE NAME

we could see them kneeling
in the pew not long after dipping
fingers in a Holy water font at the
back of the church, a little more
browned by the sun and lamenting
another Easter in the country with
English border guards always ready
to hand out more bad than good. on
their knees, they tell God in simple
words too foreign for newspaper lies
how they ran from homes carrying
a thousand village screams, never
came to take jobs, burden schools,
hospitals, tiny towns, big cities or
feel the light drained out of them by
those who never look up. we could
see them kneeling in their best dress,
walking up to the Holy Mother's altar
to light a few candles and whispering
to her they are God's unknown name
in a country with too many chains to
spare.

THE RESURRECTION

I dropped out of the eighth grade
with a needle in my veins, a library
card in my pocket and knowledge of
the names of every shooting gallery
around. my friends changed when
roaming the streets and not one of
them was like the kids at the Junior High
School studying math, dissecting frogs,
reading William Golding or getting ready
for high school entrance exams. the guys
on the street were hardened young and
near middle aged men, with scars down
their arms like a map of the barrio, all
of them graduates of Rikers Island prison
and experienced at posing for technicolor
mug shots.   my teen body trembled in
the morning like it was tapping out a
morse code to let me know it was time
for a fix, the hour to lift my legs one step
after the other down the street to hustle
up a dime for a few bags of dope to forget
the home that cast me out where a mother
occupied three rooms herself not fully alive.
on the rooftops where I shot up, before a
heroin rush washed over me, I cursed the

inheritance of the Puerto Rican Bronx with
words that would have kept local priests at
the altar rail in prayer for more than a full
year and even saying confession would fail
to make me clean with the repetitive hail
Mary and Our Father pleas. the bulldozed
building where I lived is today an empty
lot of shattered bricks with the fading sign
of the Chinese Hand Laundry, the Perez
Grocery Store, a torn New York Yankee's
banner, discarded Pampers and stray dogs
pissing on things. the hell America built
was home sweet home to me, for the murals
painted on tenement walls tourists stood in
front of taking pictures and the children on
the block that did their best to jump rope
and play.   I lived my teen years on the streets
too high to care about a damn thing, jumping
on buses to cross the country to live beside
the ocean on the West Coast and getting on
a flight to Puerto Rico to cry with my eyes
nodding out from dope beneath the columns
of a shanty town house in old San Juan. I got
used to the world looking at me sideways and
good pious church folk praying for the God
who stays away to call me home quicker than
the sanitation department would pick up the
remains of dead dogs on empty lots. today, I

think of the wrecked lives of Puerto Rican

kids, the evidence of scars on arms the color

of earth that beat too many years of dreams

into graves and finally the white working-class

family that took an interest in slowly bringing me

back to life in the name of the God of strangers,

exiles and outcasts who was hammered to a

Cross.

THE CROSS

I was unable to find my way
by simply reading the clouds
in the late afternoon, the bus
stop had a glass encased map
with names on it too difficult to
read in dim light. it was a two hour
stop on the ride across the country
but it felt like watching artificial turf
grow at the Buffalo Bills Stadium. as
we drove in and out of cities, I could
not help comparing the streets to the
ones in New York where I left a clump
of memories in the basement of Papo's
building that I knew would wait for me
to return someday.   the glassy gaze in
my fourteen-year-old junkie eyes no one
suspected on the bus was a frank way
to see the world with the transparency
never mentioned by the priests at Saint
John's Chrysostom Church. I sat in the
back of the bus quietly with my head
bowed like I was addressing God when
in fact, I was kicking dope cold turkey in
my personal freedom ride and my sick body
bore witness to the crimes of poverty and

the barbarous acts of a Christian nation too
busy with respectable white people to care
about dark families that die.

FIRE HYDRANT

morning in the hot summer
city the kids ran toward the
middle of the block to open
the fire hydrant beneath the
retreating prickly stars. the
pump tilted with play when
the Boricua boys sprayed water
at the passing bus and cars from
cans opened at both ends that
laughed at the heat wave. they
played tag in the water and ran
to the end of the street with the
sign that said Wrong Way that
no one obeyed. you could always
find Tito standing in the middle
of the street soaking wet, yelling
in Spanglish and trying to part
the water coming his way and
grinning with his whole skinny
rice and beans body. on rusted
fire escapes young mothers sat
to watch the little faces filled
with dreams and too busy to
talk about the white man who
flew to the moon and took a
Giant step for a whole bunch
of other white people.

THE LORD'S PRAYER

Our father who art in heaven
I just scored a bag of dope to
shoot into my veins in order to
nod out like it was an act of
praise. I have been wondering
about who is included in the our
of this prayer, since the good folk
at the church can't stand having
teen junkies in worship? I am sure
you know how hungry the dip and dab
teens on the streets get, how filthy the
clothes on their backs look and just to
keep things clear the neighborhood
nuns have started crossing the street
when they see us. our father in heaven
you need to walk around down here
before every kid like me vanishes from
the streets.   I know you'd like to hear
me confess something about your will
being done but damn when Rudy died
I didn't see any value in coming up with
words of concession, instead I thought
a little delivery from evil means you
confessing you forgot how to make the
world clean.   Our father when you hear

the kingdom, the power and the glory
remember us and send a sign saying the
world of misery keeping us with needles
in our veins will not last like you forever
and ever! Our God I do like to think
of you when I shoot up and sometimes
will even try to conjure your spirit to
lead me away from temptations but you
are just too slippery. our father who are
in heaven, before I nod out let me say I do
hope you remember we were born with
names!

CROOKED TEETH

the kids with God blessed crooked
teeth will never know teen life with
wires in their mouths. they will say
there is beauty in uneven teeth that
creep up the monkey bars in the little
park, jump rope in front of building
1203, get all dressed up for Sunday at
church and show something of joy at
school. they will laugh showing the
gaps in their mouths just the same while
stumbling down the sidewalk, cracking
jokes at dusk on the stoops and trying
to hide their skinny bodies behind street
lamps during hide and seek play. they
will be visited in their apartments by the
holy ghost before the year ends and fall
down in stitches when a still small voice
opens its mouth to speak some kind of old
church truth with teeth more crooked than
the back legs of the super's old hound
dog.

THE REPAIR SHOP

I remember the long summer
days where he worked out of
a closet converted into a radio
and television repair shop. he
made three kids a single transistor
radio placed in a Dick Tracy case
tinkering one afternoon. the tiny
music box looked crafted with
the invisible perfection of the FAO
Schwarz toy store downtown that
poor kids considered a labyrinth of
joy only exited by slowly walking away
backwards. on Saturday mornings,
when his work piled up, I was sent
to the local pharmacy with a bag full
of television tubes, you know the kind
resting now in peace, to test on a kit
placed in the back of the store. I liked
running that errand, the machine that
made me feel accomplished, reporting
to my father the results of the test and
watching him replace the faulty tubes
in television sets he fixed for the sake of
his neighbors' favorite Spanish language
show. he told stories then of fighting

with impoverished Indians against a
dictator in Guatemala, living for just a
few years free, escaping the terror of a
new Uncle Sam bought military regime,
walking for miles to cross a border
North, marrying a Puerto Rican teen,
joining the Navy to fight a white man's
war and finding himself full of life as a
merchant sailor on the rough seas. I
remember when he came ashore and
was too unfit to make the next ship, he
was the father that summer who fell
from the sky, the man I would never
see quite the same again. Guatemala
is still plowed for the rich, Indian blood
irrigates her fields, the widows, orphans
and lost souls still cry and I give thanks
to the absent father who gave me a tongue
to condemn in the name of God the history
that emptied his soul and brazenly crucifies
us, still!

THE BARRIO

they came with dreams that
dangled on clotheslines in lush
colors, unharmed by downtown
judgements, capturing Puerto
Rican eyes with their high wire
moves, raggedy things swaying
in the alley like my mother's hips
on the dance floor at the Hunts
Point Palace. they came with faith
dressed in garments embroidered
by abuelita hands with instructions
from heaven, worked until flesh peeled
from bone, saw children laid breathless
on sidewalks like actors in a crime scene
ribbon play and never stopped practicing
the feel, the look, the taste, the scent of new
life.   they came with kisses served up like
rice for their Spanglish speaking kids, told
them to stay out of the factories, away from
the garment district, short order cooking,
mopping floors, cleaning toilets, and taking
care of upper east side kids. the elders said
stay in school, remember the old Spanish
songs, dance salsa, cumbia, rumba, batacha,
and merengue, not waltzes. they said you will

never be laid off from these tropical dreams

that have played on the corners of the world

long before any one of us was born and the

stars were named! they said in America destiny

will tell a pack of lies but these dreams with irregular

awkward sounds that came from an island belong to

you now and will threaten you each day with life.

COQUITO

in the basement apartment, he was
preparing the cart that provided a
living that did not resemble Sunday
morning prayer. he worked hard just
to make it through each day and the
labor never did offer him a chance
to spend a day once a week in play.
in the neighborhood, he was known
as the coquito man who made Puerto
Rican ices that made mouths water
and put timbales even in the oldest
hearts. every now and then a rookie
cop dressed with a blue hat and grey
uniform from the 41st precinct would
ask to see his permit and the old man
would smile saying Jesus gave him
permission. he never got handcuffed
for selling coconut ices on the corner,
even the rookie cops knew his hard
work was in that cart and the people in
the neighborhood loved the old man
for providing a piece of the island of
enchantment to them. the old Jewish
ladies coming home with their own
two-wheeled grocery carts loved to
buy his coquito ices and sometimes
one or two talked with him about
surviving the nameless killing of
Auschwitz.

THE STORY

the world is too much with

us, it wanders the apartments,

the schools, the working day

and the places where we have

left headstones on graves. I

smell its complications in the

wind and long for a space it

cannot see us. we sit before

la Virgen de Guadalupe and

I wonder what will she do the

day our sweet words no longer

reach out to her? will she weep

into her candle for us? in the cold

empty space left will she miss

losing us? will she remember how

life in the slums that welcomed us

was made of tears?   the world has

found the moist places of our souls,

the infant face of our dreams in them

and the ancient waters they hold that

long to flow into the river Jordan.

THE WEIGHT

the words are too
heavy to speak in
the open air, they
make their way to
the Black corners
of the barrio, they
are translated into
Spanglish saying the
things English keeps
quiet. I drag them
like old letters from
absent friends to read
loudly on dark nights
to the invisible Angels
the Puerto Rican widows
tell us can be seen on the
boulevard facing the rolling
buses and noisy street kids
in the evening. the words
are heavy in every season
where no one climbs hills
with us, the nation rolls over
us and rehearses the thousands
of ways to discount us. these
words taste like years in the
making and when they finally
make noise nothing happens
and no one asks how we live
in Spanglish skin.

LOVE SONG

I walked the banks of the
East River thinking of the
day you offered a kiss to me
that disclosed right then all the
colors of the world and put a
dripping stain of love into the
Lower East Side. I never walked
the path in that little park more
gladly, dared to imagine heaven
so near and I swore seeing flowers
descending from the clouds and
altering the fragility of the world
by turning seconds into mysterious
eternity. that delicious moment has
never stopped following me even in
the dimmest light walking across the
fields of a civil war nation, beneath
the palest moon and when dancing to
celebrate the leaping beauty of this
gift called life.

THE SHOT

I clearly remember the night
you came panting from a long
painful walk out of the South
Bronx, with a lung completely
shut down by a bullet that went
clear through your thin ass wino
body and how you cried about
how people looked away when
they saw your bloody shirt. the
seminarians on the first floor
below me were busy in a Bible
study and oddly they did not
hear your shouts over their talk
and singing. I dropped bread
that was then in my hands the
moment your voice was carried
by the wind through the window
and looked out at your broken
Brown body that had all but a
crown of thorns. I rushed the
flight of stairs to the sidewalk
and put a towel on your exit
wound, held you in my arms
listening to you tell me in the
spaces between breaths how you
escaped the gun shot apartment
with just enough life to tumble
into me, afraid. we waited for
hours in the emergency room
with only one Spanish speaker,
white doctors patched you up
and we limped all the way back
to my seminary apartment where
God slept, while I wiped away
a clot of blood stuck in your

black hair and I said good to
have you home dear brother.
then, you rested and I sat under
a reading lamp pouring over the
pages of Moltmann's theology
of hope for an early morning
class.

THE GRAVES

in our hearts the tears
have fallen since the
beginning of time not
speaking English, doing
their very best to wash us
whole, shining like small
lamps with silvery moons
in them and pouring forth
with our sorrow. we stand
above these graves looking
at the brass handled boxes
of wood placed in the dark
earth, the wind blowing by
the hearse that carried God's
children to their final resting
place and taking now our tears
to the packed halls and protest
streets like letters demanding
to be read out loud. we cry
longing for these Black and
Brown bodies to resurrect in
front of our moist eyes singing
the songs America has never
heard in the places where her
invented language of hate
pretends innocence.

FIRE

the fire this time is in a
mother's tears, the hollering
blown by the wind, the young
Black boys who never grew
up to be men, the Brown sisters
not spared a grave, the ordinary
Black and Brown humanity
bad cops rushed to an end. the
fire this time is in the funeral
sermons that didn't change a
thing, the prayers of a white
nation over the ashes of the
innocent dead, the beaten who
mattered today to God, the flowers
lined up over the remains of
the gone and hope that lost its
sweet tastiness. the fire this time
cannot be fear, a rope necktie,
hate, murder, violence and rape.
the fire this time must be the
weight of Black and Brown
truth, the shriek of dark flesh,
the hands wiping away bleeding
tears and heaven letting chains
break when my people across
this fictive white earth chant
no justice, no peace.

WITNESS

I am a witness to the man
blinded by racist rage to
his white privilege who
uses every offensive word
to describe the ways he
would like to see Black and
Brown people finish on a
tree. I am a witness to the
murderous cops that laugh
about slaughtering the holy
innocence that makes a Black
martyred preacher and a slain
Brown bishop take a knee in
heaven. I am a witness to the
atrocities overlooked in the
houses of worship that never
cry rivers. I am a witness to
rotting justice, mothers who
beg for Jesus to come, kids
condemned to oblivion and
on the ancient crusted earth
the never-ending terror of white
angry men trying each day to
keep us from seeing another
rising sun. I am a witness in a
white bread world for Black
lives that matter and for the
beloved community that says
no human being is illegal no
matter how hands point to
Brown skin and angry fools
mock Spanish tongues.

THE PROSTITUTE

her name is Rosa like the
flower though her face is
a browning garden trampled
by the footsteps of tricks. she
walks beneath the Simpson
Street elevated subway forcing
a smile that she sells cheap to
men who pay more for well
dressed proper lives. she listens
to stories from those who come
from other blocks and white homes
downtown, they lay on her bed
and leave without apology.

HUSH

sleep with a night full of dreams then
wake in the morning without need of
any language. sense the colors speak,
be aware of the rustling wind and spring
to life in the common experience of a
hushed world. walk to the silent corner,
pause in the middle of the sidewalk and
interrupt the withdrawn sick, the sad and
the poor without using words. sit on the steps
of the building empty for now of all human
utterances and for once be led away to do
nothing. let the silence take you along dark
passages to light like it was a time of child's
play.

HOMESICKNESS

we need more time
that leaves us feeling
complete for the long
subway ride that ends
above ground at the park
where buses wait to take us
to the running water of the
sound where sand stitched
into a beach has held the
blankets of single mothers,
wrinkled abuelas and fatherless
children that impose sweet
laughter on the city. we need
more time to sit together to
talk about paradise in la Santa
biblia and to imagine in a loud
voice heaven a place to embrace
once again lost family and friends
still deeply loved. we need more
time to misplace hard days like
kids lost to the world on carousel
rides with songs never heard. we
need more time to ride the first
subway car looking down the old
tracks and listening to the train
blow its horn to rout the pigeons
from them and have the sight fill
us with the lyrics nostalgic for a
lost country and declaring in a
borrowed tongue that this new
country is home.

AMERICA

we walked slowly to
the other side with bad
news following us and
long messages pinned on
walls and church doors
waiting for us with more
of it. for several months,
we never left the room by
day aware there was no such
thing as a straight line to a
new life. twenty years later
nothing has changed, there
are no fairy tale moments to
write about to the old country
and our greatest possession is
fear of a workplace raid, waking
too early for Mass, being brutally
beaten for speaking Spanish in
public and listening to the moans
of our children born here and
limping each day of life on these
shores. we ask too often when will
America stop beating us to our knees?
when does the welcome begin? When
will freedom and equality so hushed
these days be ours?

BABEL

in your America, the politics of hate
works the halls of government with
dangerous tribalism, fueled by white
lies told by the minute that build walls
to stop the advance of inclusive equality
and every dream worthy of this place
called a nation.   in your America, the
nightly news rushes into living rooms
to say another young Black man was
killed by an authority paid to protect
him, Brown children were arrested for
crossing the border by agents that never
appeared in their innocent dreams and
the world we are crushed in is distant
from everything about you save the old
white loathing responsible for the theft
of ancient lands, the slaughter of men,
women and children of every first nation
and the systematic lynching of Black
humanity enslaved for many American
centuries by plantation owners whose
portraits hang in the finest government
offices.   in your America, I visited a
pretty white church where a sweet old
woman read scripture from the Hebrew
prophet Amos cherished by our martyred
Martin the words that said, hate evil, love
good; maintain justice in the courts. I
could not help turning my head to the left
to whisper into the ear of my suspect citizen
son the words of the writer who told the
truth on the mountain top, America has been
white too long to listen!

DAGGERS

the color of hate has taught
me too many things about
the country that has invested
so heavily in American ropes
made ironically by the dark
hands of the country where
I was born. I would like to
point to the apartments
that shelter us but I am
more familiar with trees,
rusty nails, thrown stones
and the spots where people
in the silenced places sit telling
tales as Black tears pour down
their cheeks. you see, the
color of unforgettable loathing
makes us tremble to the bone
and turns us into something not
us. come, stand in our worn out
shoes in the broad light of day and
perhaps then you will not think
our speeches, hollering and long
marches are confused.

ADAM TOLEDO

the world ended in an
alley for a thirteen year
old Mexican-American
boy when a raging white
cop pulled his pistol out
and shot this child with
both hands raised dead
but the ears cut off by
the police propaganda
office manufactured a
different story about the
horror committed by a
white man with a badge.
when the boy was chased
into the alley he felt it could
be his final breath and the
world made in the image
of the cop would not call
it murder. Adam Toledo
died once in that alley and
we have died more than a
thousand times in the last
year at the hands of men
and women who don't give a
shit about Black and Brown
lives. mothers are begging
for their children, our night
sweats leave us drenched
and there is no escaping the
hell that carves its initials
on our dark backs! fuck,
the least I can do is never
let your white world forget
its sin!

AGAIN

I hear people say let us take this
moment to pray for yet another
young Black man shot to death
by a cop offering excuses that
will not bring back Daunte from
the dead. what love brought into
this world racist hate has undone
and the litany of young Black
lives laid into silent graves is
the final word about why trusting
a badge on a uniform dressing a
white face is fatal. in America,
dying wears a Black and Brown
face at traffic stops and all the
places the crooked politicians,
errant cops and the silent majority
declare to never mind. in America,
I hear the men, women and children
who deserved to live crying from
beneath the earth justice cannot
breathe and never did for those who
stroll away after dancing around
the sundry lynching trees.

INFERIOR SCHOOLS

the classrooms in my South Bronx
schools were filled with Black and
Brown faces never mentioned in the
required reading lifting up white voices
like that history never leaped out of hell
and lynched us to trees. I never heard
teachers mention shackled dark America,
the places beyond Jerusalem where Christ
goes on being killed, slave auctions, ethnic
genocide, four Black girls murdered in a
church, the young Black and Brown boys
policed into graves and the nation's old
White House built on stolen earth. you see,
the beginning these teachers in my public
school wanted us to believe was nothing
but white and silence for all other colors.
bullshit, we said. there never was or will be
an America without us and shit even the
Bible that has made frequent appearances
over the last 250 or so years on this land is
not white and doesn't speak American English.

HEART

every infant heart

is beating today

like before time

was invented and

these Brown kids'

innocent lips taste

milk with their first

breath held in young

mothers' arms whose

dark eyes have darling

written on them. Angels

come to see for themselves

these faces that will never

hide in the city and will

learn to appropriate the

English phrases that will not

permit them to be cancelled

out by the smug citizens who

forget they too are caught

between the beginning and

the end. I am pleased to see

them grow, to spread across

the earth and confess the world

is a beautiful place even when

entered from hell!

AWAKE

leave the window
open tonight when
the tenement sleeps,
wait patiently to see
if the souls talked of
in the church around
the corner come for a
visit. carefully make
out the faces to see if
you recognize anyone
and remember all the
smiles you lost on the old
city block. listen carefully
to the voices that speak
in the dark to chase away
the inquisitive hours of
bitter days when you ask
why God created.

LOVE

I have softly whispered
about you calling out to the
voyaging clouds that know
nothing of borders and are
full of laughter from lands
that God made to speak in
Spanish. I dreamed on the
lonely streets of your long
brown hair, beautifully baked
skin and the many ways you
delivered me from the valley
of sighs. my heart beats with
endless desire in the time that
burns away these days, louder
than the hour Christ was born
and dancing at the sweet sound
of your name and the gracious
gifts of everything you give.

CITY OF GOD

this city with apartments
under furnished, crowded
with children that move
each morning to look out
of windows, where each
occupant remembers only
in Spanish, walks each
day in old shoes and hides
in shadows has heard last
prayers far too many days
in a row. I sat in a church
smelling the fumes of a
passing bus and hearing
the shouting voices of the
Puerto Rican girls leaving
the Perez stationer's and
asked God to speak less
English and confess we
were all born here, learned
America's alphabet, twisted
her English on our tongues
and sampled white hands
casually beating dear life
out of us.

LAST WORD

the children of the war
only have Brown faces
and names too difficult
to say in this country. you
know, teachers in middle
school sometimes project
a map on a screen for a class
lesson with an outline of the
tiny country that cost the USA
billions of dollars to almost
kill. I hate that they always
forget to mention the mothers
of the Brown faced kids who
were among the millions of
poor that only God saw. I recall
running away from soldiers in
a tiny mountain village and
thinking about the many times
I heard white pastors and highly
educated theologians say God
loves you, while Uncle Sam
taxes busily made big holes in
Brown bodies. I confess it was
a terrifying time and no winged
Angels swooped down to scoop
any of us up and that heaven talked
about in so many churches and
academic halls always managed
not to send an ambassador of
Christ to weep with the poor. I
still carry the faith of my burnt
people and consider it a very
special inheritance but each
day leaves me less convinced
God made Brown for love.

COLD DAY MEMORIES

I was just twelve unable
to hear the singing birds,
no longer keen to play in
little kid games and finding
my way to the corners that
served the junkie herd on the
block with dope. I confess
thinking my birth certificate
on the hard-living streets did
not mean a damn thing and
the melancholy song always
popping in my head replete
with the self-pitying words
that described me to be just
another throwaway Puerto
Rican kid was as unworthy
of a newspaper story or the
local church's time as Joseph's
death from a rooftop OD. I
belonged to the subtle spell
of the junkie corner then, the
white powder that made me
an abandoned tenement short
order cook and the neighborhood
that even God I often suspected
forgot existed. I lived mighty
long years on the street that
cold days even now bring up
to my throat that once swallowed
English from an old television
set in the place I use to call
home. I have been arrested
by white policemen in a college
town for being myself, learned
quickly in higher education that

speaking English does not make
you more American, made peace
with the darkness of youth and
curse often at the profanities
of a nation that keeps sticking a
needle in my veins and tells me
that is freedom!

LOISAIDA RENAISSANCE

when you get off the subway
to make your way into the East
Village if you want to smell
flowers you should have stayed
in Connecticut. some folks like
to tour these streets chasing the
ghosts of Auden, O'Hara, and
Ginsburg from Saint Mark's
Church-in-the-Bowery to the
haunts that sheltered the cheap
rent white poets who engaged
politics, morals, religion and
love with their white pens. as
you make the tour walk over
to Avenue D shake from your
head every white thought and
listen to the Black and Brown
lips that have never been wrong
about the white world's failure
to see. the heavy Black and
Brown presence of the East
Village poetry scene is not in
the poetry tour package you
see but the people who live
on the Alphabet streets know
Amiri Baraka, Hettie Jones,
Pedro Pietri, Miguel Piñero,
Sandra María Esteves and the
birthplace of the Nuyorican
Renaissance that will come into
light the longer you walk on the
other side with the poets who
have been busy rearranging the
American dream.

THE COLD

when it became cold in the apartment
and it was clear the landlord turned off
the heat to save money, the kitchen
burners were fired and we all gathered
dressed with the rags once called clothing
around the stove to warm. talking was a
pretty misty affair when exhaled words
condensed in the cold air fogging up my
sister's glasses. how odd that the uptown
landlord found time to send the message
that rent was due in English and Spanish
just in case, though most of the people in
the building hardly read in either one of the
two and bloodshot Mr. Ira coming round to
knock on doors never got the message out
of his mouth cause people were yelling in
plain court room English, heat! the people
in the next-door apartment who shared the
fifth floor with other poor ranting sofrito
beings had the nerve to say in the best broken
English I ever heard nothing much has changed
for us in this God smothered country. shit, I
am still shivering those days no matter where
I go and find the only way to make the memories
warm is to stand on the avenue with my dark
kin who fill the earth way beyond those cheap
landlords most exclusive dreams.

RUNNING COLD

it was a single-digit morning,
the road a sheet of white with
tire marks sweeping left and
right on the empty streets. on
tree limbs the ice crystals that
had formed overnight reflected
the distant winter sun warming
ever so slightly the wind. each
step planted on the wintry vigorous
earth in this simple morning run
wearing layers of clothing that
weighed more than me eased my
soul by letting me see the whole
world, cold and warm, silent and
noisy, broken and perfect, joyous
and blue right in front of me and
wholly in plain view. over the last
few miles of the run, my thumbs
cold with protest, I finished the
laps through the neighborhood
with Ahmaud Arbery who last
year was shot and killed while
out running by two white men
at the tender age of 25. when
I got home there was a knot in
my throat and a few tears frozen
on my checks that spilled for the
matter of truth!

CHILD, DONE

they crossed the border a
little more wrinkled than
yesterday into a world made
up of illegals since the days of
conquest. there wasn't a child
among them that did not know
the meaning of leaving home
behind, a mother who did not
weep with longing for the parted
country full of violence nor friends
who would not recognize their new
English names. they crossed into
the world that calls them nothing,
arroz-con-pollo wetbacks, rice and
bean spics and Brown people the
hate-drunk white country never cared
to love. they crossed the border with
their hungry lives, ready to take the
worst jobs without complaint, see kids
attend the shitty schools preparing them
for 15 years to life and experience their
dark flesh mutilated by white lies that
passed for insight about migrants. I will
never forget the sight of the cheap wood
coffin lid closing while death played in
the neighborhood where the teen boy who
walked in it was labeled in the new just
another Hispanic killed by a county cop for the
crime of keeping his Brown hand in a pocket
in front of his abuela's building. Shit, his name
was Tito!

UNEMPLOYED

I walked into the restaurant
where two middle aged men
sat at the counter talking about
how they were now sons of
unemployment and needed to
select cheap from the menu.
they arrived in the city many
years earlier from a land that
hears radios moan in Spanish
and where people have stopped
thinking about them. they left
everything that mattered in that
faraway place, memories, joys,
torments and their deepest reasons
for living. you could see once they
had a different face, not a bitter
word jumped out from the hidden
parts of their hearts and they never
expected to settle into a bandaged
existence in a crooked country that
only lets them be two faceless
bodies in need of work.

SILENCE

tonight, when the
city lights brighten
the dark, the moon
is hardly visible and
only a single star is
viewed, we will pray
to the massive mystery
named in many tongues
and beyond the rambling
cultures that so thoroughly
limit us. tonight, tirelessly
we will search for warmth,
look for signs spreading
across the sky from distant
heaven and move well into
another day when the clocks
nudge us back to dull and
muddled understanding. tonight,
what can be more regrettable
than not surrendering to the
myths that give us life and the
the attractive silence.

FROZEN

the cold winter, the
crying poor, the women,
children, elderly and ill
will holler into the homes
of callous politicians louder
by the hour that God's judgment
is on their fancy heads. the
calm features of the Methodist
Bishops, the crooked silence
of the earthly church, the glossy
scriptures that only come out
to wish the innocent everlasting
rest will be driven by the wind
that carries the world's pain to
the land where truth cannot be
deceived. today, we know the
name of the frozen child pursued
one night by death and he leaves
the government and quiet church
undone.

CENSUS-TAKER

the old census taker came
knocking on the door just
when the baby in the back
room started to cry. for the
census agent the infant was
a number to be collected, a
resident in the building of
a neighborhood in waste, a
body caught with others in
the early morning hours and
a sign of the browning of the
country. the malnourished trees
in the little park whose leaves
had dropped knew the names
of everyone in the household
and posed for pictures with them
the day the infant was baptized
in the church that hasn't seen a
white face in forty years. the
census man had no idea the
family in the apartment came
from a land in ruins for hundreds
of years and aged by the violence
that crossed the sea. he knocked
again on the door only hoping for
the accuracy that would give the
nameless a place.

SHORT-ORDER COOK

on First Avenue in what the
papers call the East Village
a Puerto Rican man who is
working the grill in a Ukrainian
restaurant knows he lives on the
Lower East Side of Manhattan. he
makes breakfast every day of the
week for white lawyers, doctors,
bankers, brokers, artists and University
rich kids that come into the place
mornings and especially on quiet
Sundays with whiskey, beer and
rum still rolling in their bellies. they
have no idea what happens between
Avenues A and D, never think about
the priests still saying Mass at the Lady
of Sorrows Church excluding the language
of redemption for those not their kind
like spics, streetwalkers and the beloved
humanity coming out in the name of
love. after serving messy eggs all morning,
he gets off work, walks to a tiny apartment
on Avenue D and is pleased by the sight
of Spanglish speakers on the street who know
the wretched of the earth are blessed. when
justice rolls down like water, perhaps his
white neighbors will unclog their ears to
hear him shout life is not meaningless for
the people they have long said are no more
than undeserving spics!

NUYORICAN

we marked the evening having
a very long abstract conversation
into the dullest region of intellectual
deliberation where you went on about
the poem Puerto Rican Obituary written
by my dear friend the late Pedro Pietri.
ordinarily, I would have requested you
talk a long walk in Central Park talking
to yourself until reaching the North end
of it where Spanish Harlem sings every
night about the five characters in the
poem. yes, the people that in your long
academic disquisition you oddly forgot
to say never talk back, always get to work
on time and keep their Spanish names. I
wanted to interrupt your NYU speech to
say like Pietri I saw more than a few of
these good people die and no matter how
long you talk comfortably from the café
chair you will not understand the babies
crying, the shit paid for hard work, bullets
flying, cop baton beatings, kids in school
pledging allegiance to the nation that kills
them nor a single dream from the hearts
found in our diasporic slums.

QUO VADIS, MIGUEL

they burned wood in an old
barrel on a rooftop while standing
around it talking in a low voice
of biblical proportion about the
the Lower East Side and Miguel's
ashes scattered in it. they wondered
in broken English about his soul
floating to a different shore or
what remained of him on the
broken streets. the curling blue
smoke rose above their heads,
drifted toward the East River
and Tito called it an omen that
their friend's weightless spirit
was by then headed to heaven.
the churro cart vendor in front
of the local Catholic church
waited for parishioners to exit
to make sales and one of the guys
mumbled covered by smoke the
block has a new pope. the barrio
will not be the same with Miguel
gone but perhaps these fresh corrido
residents will write a song about
him.

TOMORROW

tomorrow, I would like to see
the world with the Spanish kids
drawing straight lines on Walls
and with steady voices declaring
nothing is wrong. tomorrow, I
would like to open my eyes after
a night full of the wildest dreams
to say to anyone who will listen the
other side of the world is not at all
dark and side streets only lead to
the dead ends where you will find
La Virgen de Guadalupe waiting
with a smile. tomorrow, I want to
slowly walk on enchanted streets,
make my way down to the East River
to watch it nudge the shore and feel
happiness seeing chubby pigeons on
the fire escapes of old buildings that
are thick with the sound of Spanglish
that is too spicy for the conscientious
purists in America and on the other
side of the bogus line. tomorrow, I
would like to pull down heaven from
the sky, hold it like a candle-flame on
the block and spend the day playing
children's games until God is restless
enough to kneel.

THE SOUTHERN GATE

my father was an undocumented
immigrant, a young border crosser
with Mayan blood rushing through
his veins, fleeing a land owned by
the wealthy, worked by Indians for
centuries that were always pursued
by the grave, exiled from his country
for good, emptying every adult year
for America by fighting in its second
world war and sailing the seas on her
ships. I watched him try to restart his
heart in the country that told him get
out, felt his humanity perish when he
turned in the night beating his children
and wife and asked every tear that rolled
down my face when will the government
agree it cannot exist without people like
us. yes, this man was undocumented to
the bone when he crossed the border into
Texas in the 1930s, when workplace raids
were only rumored, God spoke up in churches
against la migra and Jesus tied him here to
life. I will always hold on to my old man's
broken English dream, forgive him family
transgressions and find him in the world of
strangers walking me daily to the southern
gate of heaven.

GOD TOO SMALL

the old newspapers held in a
bundle by frayed rope, filled
with the afflicted stories of the
nation, straddling the years that
you have grown up, sit like these
times in a dark closet. the hours
slip away naked into spaces no
longer counting time, impossible
to think, while you look out the
window at places between buildings
finding the light causing the dark
to depart a bitter Sunday. you think
about Gypsy your transgender friend
who performs in night clubs, appeared
in a couple of movies and has a PhD
in Russian literature but was never hired
by a university to teach Chekhov. you look
up at the clouds floating by slowly over
the building roof mumbling how cruel
progressive democracy, theology and
the prudish voyeurs of life repeatedly
fail to embrace Gypsy and find him
above all guilty. after a short period
of silence, you decide to invent a few
prayers for the gods too small to love
and against the stupidity inventing hell
on earth.

SCHOOL DAYS

a pair of socks are drying on the
radiator breathing loudly for the
entire night and the foggy bedroom
window twists the faces of people
on the street before the church bells
start their ringing. a small flock of
black sparrows balance together
on the sill complaining of a cold
wind that blows across the alley
and granting observers a few minutes
of unforeseen grace. soon, he will slip
on yesterday's socks in a corner of
the room, head down the stairs from
the fifth-floor sneezing in Spanglish
until reaching the sidewalk where he
will stroll to school, swear allegiance
to the shadows on the assembly room
flag and absorb his lessons with the
seventh grade manners bursting with
a baseball stadium of opinions. at the
end of the public-school day, he will
make his way back to apartment 5C
to recite lines from Black and Brown
poets the white teachers ignored to
please the whiney white kids.

THE RAID

while they worked cleaning
office building floors tired of
heavy mops they imagined the
cornfields back home, the ocean
air and lush green mountains that
welcomed them. in the garment
warehouses they gladly recall the
tender Spanish of grandmothers
who braided kids' hair for school
and hours to daydream without ever
feeling terrified about workplace
raids that round up Brown bodies
for an old-fashioned God bless America
back of the damn bus stoning. they
slipped by the wall, learned to keep
a step ahead of the border guards and
live in shadows where English prayers
have little reach. Lord, by the waters
of Babylon, they lament!

HOPE

we live changing a little
each day with our concerns,
transgressions, obsessions,
dreams and sins. we drift in
seconds, hours, days, weeks,
months and years trying hard
not to lose sight of a way out
of the dark. we wander in a
wilderness of untamed logic
aimless with ritual piety and
unkept promises. we weep with
others about a man with pierced
flesh and find hope creeping along
with the wind.

DISINHERITED

there is a middle-aged beggar
sitting on the church steps with
other dreams. he walks up to the
sanctuary door every Sunday but
never comes in. at night, you can
see him asleep beneath the silent
moon and contemplative stars on
the same steps and no one has ever
wondered why good news can't
reach him. around the corner, there
is a drunk holding a bottle of Midnight
Express cheap wine, repeating his first
lost day, beyond the homilies in the
church that never once has bothered
to write his name. in the middle of
the block, there is an elderly woman
sitting in front of a closed restaurant
trembling alone with the disquiet of
silence that has been with her long
enough to make God an orphan of truth
and promises of salvation.

LA COLONIA

when the gangs came to the
Colonia, the teen bread seller on
his bicycle was making rounds,
grandmothers were up early to
make breakfast and kids climbed
into uniforms for school. that day
school lessons focused on national
geography, how many volcanoes
stretched across the country, the
simple beauty of the ocean, valleys
and mountain peaks. the playground
was crowded with children kicking
a soccer ball, girls huddled in one
corner laughing at the time of day,
and teachers walking about with
bones rattling like the wind pushing
dead leaves. then, the gangs that haunted
us in dreams, lived each day beneath
our skin and terrified our mothers, took
possession of the neighborhood to squeeze
money out of the poor. they raped and
killed a thirteen-year-old sister who stayed
home that morning to help an abuela who had
gone to the market. the mothers could not
drive away the terror from a single heart, they
stayed up until morning light talking of flight
and could only think of leaving the customized
gang graves with every step north.

PIGEONS

the pigeons came to rest
on the fire escape today
after migrating south from
Columbus Circle. the little
group balanced on the iron
rails cried in the whistling
wind while the playful Puerto
Rican kids ran up and down
on the sidewalk collecting
their precious tears. little
Ana could not stop looking
at them while she thought
in the fading light as the first
stars appeared beckoning her
to heaven how beautiful were
the birds that came to visit the
tenement known for sorrow.
they let their tears fall flatly
on the sidewalk and like us
longed for those missed on
the other side of the border,
on rocks still in the water of
a distant sea and from corners
on the block.

SPANISH MOON

the block in this aging city
is never quiet save when
the leaves rustle on the
trees in the park where
migrants sit to smell the
night. the children on the
sidewalks are pushed by
the strong breezes into the
alleys to battle imaginary
dragons threatening nightly
to swallow the moon. the
people here find hundreds of
ways to turn the concrete walks
into a landscape of laugher and
happiness believed like in no
other parts of town. I will never
leave this place no matter how
far away and shall always hold
its dreams until my very own
last quiet night!

THE MIGRANTS

no matter how far you walk,
the cost of the faux papers to
give you passage, the years of
saving to pay for the trip, the
border guards you manage to
evade in the middle of the night,
when you cross the star mangled
border tenderness will be cornered
far away behind you. no matter the
news of abuela lapsed into illness,
the long-term shame of the mouthless
people and the presence of a country
full of insulting language, you will
find in the mornings that shyly come
to beckon you back to the hard day
of bent work a reason to hold hands
with the people in shantytowns, refugee
camps, barrios, Colonias, ghettos and
slums who carry the word home deep
in their souls. no matter how much you
wish to hurry up the dreams that helped
you make it this far do not forget what
you imagined no matter what the white
privileged say.

THE COLD

that winter city trucks
plowed snow into small
mountains on the Avenue,
the Apartments shivered
and the complaints came
in English, Yiddish, Italian
and Spanish. in the hallways
people gathered like it was
a day at the United Nations
to tell stories they had waited
long to unfold and the ghosts
of those unable to tremble sat
in the stairwells leaning into
the conversations. by seven
o'clock the Catholic School
kids in their fine used uniforms
begin to exit their homes with
backpacks filled with scarcely
read books, sometimes a rosary
and freezing beliefs. they smile
like kids who know hard working
mothers will make their way to
light candles in church for them
giving thanks for having too little
of anything and a whole lot of life.
then, young grandmothers make an
entrance in the tenement halls on their
way to the Bodega complaining about
the South Bronx and its cousin slums in
places around the globe that have iron chains
for dark people who stubbornly push freedom
into the spaces they live with five loaves and
two fish.

THE POETS CAFÉ

when I walk by the old café
dreaming of the old days inside
where wood floors creaked and
poets long gone with soft dark
eyes read lines from a latest work
that paced the world in words, I
must tell you the sadness drops
from my graying hair. when I make
my way to the disfigured park beside
the East River, the bench that waited
for you each day to empty a brown heart
of the poetry that taught the Spanglish
souls living in the projects how to sing,
dance and even pray, I can say my aging
soul leaves the wilderness for several
hours each day. when I see your name
graffitied on walls of the near abandoned
streets of lower Manhattan, surrounded by
images I have seen in the city and watched
gallop toward heaven, I am beckoned by
signs of aging to Thompkins Square Park
to stand beside the tree shedding leaves to
protest the drowning of the innocent and
to ask about the second coming that will
deliver the world from the clutches of the
rich who steal life from people with too
little.

UNSTAINED

one night in the exalted city
shining in the dark the dreams
in all the apartments somehow
became mine. I cannot tell you
why I sat for hours on the stoop
pondering the future made from
old history scattered like dust on the
streets with candles on each corner
where you could hear the breathing of
widows from open windows uniting
with that of the dead. I waited for a
light to streak across the cloudy night
sky writing in Spanish for all the world's
streets to see, to promise the sad eyes
with simple words a new day, the desire
in hearts to hope and walks with Brown
flesh people speaking in tongues unstained
by English. after talking with Lela one
night, I was reminded of the fragile paradise
no one ever found climbing the Statue of
Liberty, in prayer at the local church,
disclosed by evening news or hiding in
the specks of dust blown by the wind into
the East River. I confessed to dearest Lela
paradise is this precious life cannot be found
on a map and it is the mischief already filling
us with life.

THE LATE SHOW

precious Lord in the basement of
this church where we listen to the
old moaning out loud about having
too much of nothing and we keep asking
when will you take our hand to lead
us into the promised land?   we heard
you engraved our Spanish names in
that faraway place of provisions for
the tired and people who look just like
the freed slaves who crossed the Red
Sea. precious Lord can you hear us
moaning, cursing, stuttering, aching and
dying in cheap creaking beds? when will
you come to the block, drift into apartments
like sunlight on a chilly Spring Day and
let your Spirit drop from heaven to calm
the trembling lips that never stop saying you
have forgotten about selfless love and have
no regard for spics. precious Lord, for too
long we have lived behind barbed wire with
the aroma of flowers from the white side of
the world and all we ask now is for you to
come near to whisper in our ears we are not
far from your freedom land.

THE WAILING

in the morning the kids
without friends in schools
that without end tell them
you are not white enough
to play, too dumb to learn
and dark to belong know a
white Jesus does not answer
prayers and he only delivers
the same old lousy peace. the
kids written about in fancy wise
books, trashed by the prosperity
preachers, locked away by bribed
judges, rotting for years in white
jails in the name of unequal laws,
sticks and stones breaking their
heads will someday be set free to
march upright in the name of the
young lives that died from land theft,
in middle passage, slavery, Auschwitz
and by the hand of the wealthy who
sponsored every war on earth. yes, in
the morning the kids who wail will not
ever let anyone forget they are still here
and one day they will laugh loud enough
to seduce heaven down to earth and things
will never be the same!

MY NAME IS NOT SPIC

I cannot change the hours
spent alone on the streets,
the bullets once dodged, knives
that were plunged into me, my
Puerto Rican and Guatemalan flesh,
the languages I speak, the years lived
with a loathed last name and life
with the dark humanity counted in
America among the wrong people who
live. you will find my sad story told in
the history of mothers raped, Indians
hunted by Catholic Spaniards, Africans
enslaved, armies occupying conquered lands,
military regimes getting big fat checks from
Uncle Sam, city hospital medical crimes, the
coast-to-coast unemployment line, schools
that fail, rocks thrown at the border Wall and
the jails too long full up. you know its time you
learn my name is not Spic and deactivate your
depravity by simply confessing King said it in
Puerto Rico and Romero refused to allow bullets
to erase it.

POLICE BRUTALITY

the cops who drop us to the
ground delighting in every

Black and Brown throat they
crush with a knee inside of

a blue trouser on a neck will
not find peace in God even

though they have a whole lot
of mostly white citizens that

come to their defense. you
know these public servants

murder us for writing bad
checks, running a stop sign,

taking a run along the public
streets of a posh community,

sitting on a park bench in quiet
prayer, strolling the parking lot

of a mall, leaving a swimming
pool, exiting a church service,

walking a family dog and even
when sitting in our own living

rooms. not even God can return
to us what is lost, the courts find

ways to put those killed on trial
but insist society be kind to the

good old boys in blue who take
a life and cause the sobbing of

parents, relatives, friends and
even Christ. listen up buried

between the pages of books, the
back of the newspaper and court

files are the truths that denounce
the white social theater that never

looks at us and uses the courts
to kill Black and Brown humanity

again and again. it's time for the
cops with crooked smiles, judges

who defend white criminality and
preachers full of shit about how

things go down in our bitter world
to hear us when we march in protest

and read the ancient words of the
Hebrew prophet: hate evil; love

good; maintain justice in the
courts.

GOOD FRIDAY

there are many roads to take
in the country with so many who
scratch their heads at the site of
people with beautifully dark skin
and not one of them leads to the
promised land. there are too many
citizens you see imagining a day
without my Black and Brown people
walking the streets, harvesting crops,
building houses, cooking food, caring
for innocent white kids and cleaning filth.
that day will never come says the good
Lord who does not speak English and is
never seen by the Dixieland souls beating
him in the Good Friday flesh of all his
colored earthly kin. there are many roads in
the country and if you listen to hollering
on them you cannot miss the voices of
the crucified not silenced. we walk the
highways and byways you see asking the
bastard Christ who was lynched on a tree
to grant us love and courage to shiver with
him until all the blind can see!

THE HORROR

they spread the table of
injustice in the name of
a killer cop and centuries
without softness grab us
by the throat in one more
wicked gesture to make us
all stop breathing. they put
the victim on trial for drug
abuse to convince the world
it was fentanyl and not a bad
white cop who took a Black
man's life. we watch yet another
lobotomized American court unfold
the white show with the customary
smoke and mirrors in strategic place
that alone work their blinding charm
in the name of a twisted God and
ornamental authority. we watch
each day carefully wiping the crap
from our eyes and washing our Black
and Brown ears that are licked with
lies told by lawyers, judges and the
union of police. we hope! we view!
we expect justice to claim hold of
the hateful executioner who once
wore blue.

SIMPLE

I like sitting on a bench at
the lake feeling a soft breeze
emerge from the distant shore
and hearing your voice in the
silence. my eyes linger in the
quiet of the immense morning
and the tears in them see those
who suffer in a world waking
up bent. I see other witnesses
out for a stroll along the banks
of the lake and feel compelled
to spell out the names of those
abandoned by light but birds on
a tree branch singing about love
stop me. I stay in the park for
a little while longer listening to
the English words given to me
by a rejecting society that flutter
about in my head like dragonflies
over water and nevertheless confess
the time is ever so sweet.

RUDY

it was cold on the streets,
you never saw a cozy Grand
Concourse apartment and
cheap wine warmed your
blood better than Sunday
words that said you belong
to God. I cannot tell you
how much your broken life
weeping in the laundromat
surrounded by hellish junkies
cracking jokes has meant to
me after thirty-six years of
absence. that Easter evening
you died a strong rain kept me
company all the way to the city
morgue to which I was called
to identify your remains, after
your exhausted body was found
stretched out on Walton Avenue,
lifeless. I prepared your funeral,
dressed you in my only suit for
church, tucked my ordination
Bible beneath your left arm, kissed
you on the forehead, whispered see
you later into your ear and let a
tear the sweet Lord put in my eye
for the wretched of the earth drop
on your cheek. man, I cried and
haven't stopped since and sweet
brother when I finally make the last
pilgrimage to see you it will be with
this inescapable wailing living in my
soul.

EASTER SUNDAY

I have walked for hours
across the city, passed the
old fountain in Washington
Square Park, certain I would
not find Angels on the stroll
and another Easter would require
the good Lord to approach
me like disbelieving Thomas
in the upper room. when I made
it to the Bowery that once long
ago was called skid row wino
footsteps said far more than all
the homiletical explaining that
assured the faithful in church
while neglecting to mention
beggars, prostitutes, junkies,
drunks and tormented people
who do not appreciate Christ's
disappearing act. I bumped into
crossdressing Gypsy on Bleecker
Street who said smiling that he
preferred last supper evenings
but looked forward to a full
drag Easter Sunday. I was on a
pilgrimage to the very tip of
Manhattan Island that day imagining
Easter might convince me life was
not a disease. I finally reached Battery
Park and watched a few boats going
North on the Hudson River and I just
waited praying for the mute God to
send a sign.

RISEN

in that desolate country
on the wood where you
died and water did not
touch your lips to quench
thirst you were taken down
and laid in a tomb. poor
travelers who heard of it
wept until they caught the
good news you have risen
for them and us. your blood
was poured for all the places
life turns to dust, to end the
wars planting crosses on this
great earth, for the weak and
stout errant who need your
news of beating death. today,
you do not live in our sorrow
but have risen on this land to
bring us down from the razing
crosses and show us the way
to the place worldly hate and
death cannot visit.

SCIENCE CLASS

it happened in science class
in the 8th grade where a teacher
with emerald green eyes talked
to a room full of Puerto Rican
students, the children of the great
diaspora from the Caribbean
island whose parents did not
travel gladly to New York. the
way her eyes danced around
the classroom carefully landing
on the fragile Brown teen faces,
then how they widened descending
with questions for students opened
us with kindness for study. on the
day the voice in her eyes talked to
us, I felt the varied carols of America
singing as Whitman said but this time
in a school room on 179th Street in a
neighborhood with English fading for
over a decade. it happened in a science
class held on the second floor of an old
school building on a block where nothing
good was ever expected, our souls burned
bright, the lessons we had learned on the
far side of the city about hate crumbled
and we detected simple thoughts let a
whole lot of beauty in.

OUR COUNTRY

there are lawmakers with the
imbecilic idea that immigrants
with a dark shade of skin are
criminals, rapists, drug dealers,
worthless paupers, beggars too
physically and mentally diseased
to belong to the white stock of
a nation born from colonialism,
indigenous genocide, slavery and
and theft. the voices that navigated
the seas, the farms, the construction
projects, the roads, the schools, the
border and even the cries of a colored
man nailed to a cross though loud
have been told for centuries you do
not belong. time for heaven to rain
on that Lilly white parade to have
all the foolish people too bleached
to see their racist alphabet will never
make a sentence spit out truth and the
wide American earth will never stop
being populated with God's flowering
from every race who are not frightened
by idiots full of terror, violence and
hate.   malefactors let me whisper in
your pale ears this is our beautiful
country and your latest brownshirt
will become powder on your backs
on your way to nowhere!

DAWN

we marched a long way to
reach tomorrow bright all
day.

the other life known by every
yesterday is far behind us with
time quitting work.

today we will slowly ride the
wind with not a single bashful
dream refused.

CATECHISM

I will tell you that on
the way to Catechism
class with the old Irish
priest the Puerto Rican
boys holding their book
of lessons unread never
understood why going to
church on Sunday, saying
prayers and singing hymns
that crossed the Atlantic
mattered. once a week they
left school early for religious
instruction where the word
of God meant memorization
and forty lashes if you did not
behave. they were not sure
faith would be worth too many
years of their lives especially
given the far-off look on the
decent folks faces and even the
priest when they questioned why
God has not even lifted a finger
to save Angel from getting shot
over a ten-dollar bag of dope or
why the hand of God did nothing
to keep their mothers from being
felt up at work by fat old white
men. together they laughed about
growing up in a world that asked
them to accept too many things
but they had to draw the line on
the harsh heavenly gate that
despite all the candles lighted
for the Saints in the resonant
dark the sanctuary was always

closed to people like them who
spent their days gasping for
air. nevertheless, they made
it to Catechism class and so
many mothers were happy
when they received their first
communion though God said
nothing.

THE PIT

in the kitchen on the window
sill there is a jar with an avocado
pit that is talked to each morning
in Spanish. three toothpicks like
the Trinity around the rim of the
jar suspend it and everyone in the
apartment wants to see how it will
end. its root has not sunken into
a dark ground and sometimes even
prayers to our own gods are said for
it with stories of the trees in line on
another piece of earth that speaks
the avocado language. we admire the
perfect life quietly unfolding by the
window, watching a mother braid
a little girl's hair for school in the
stalled seconds of the city that have
learned to roam the streets consoling
strangers. perhaps, the pit is a thing
from heaven and that is why it can
hear the pleas of mothers who visit
regularly to say the Rosary and wear
out the unseen ears of the flowering
pit with long stories.

EL BARRIO

out of the darkness
the voice came to
whisper words it has
taken too long to get
here. a hand tenderly
stroked my face like
a blessing delivered
in Eden. in the dark I
fumbled for words in
the two languages given
to me by a mother and
public schools and then
confessed the new light
in the room. I was the
child not afraid, the one
noticing the salsa playing
on Tremont Avenue stores,
the kid who stared at the big
dark eyes of the Puerto Rican
sisters living on the fifth floor,
the grandmother who cared for
them and the poor old men with
their rerun lives. I can now tell
you hope that night came out of
darkness and I have tasted it again
and again, in every painted dream
that traveled the long distance from
ancient lands to the apartment in
this Spanglish slum.

IMAGINE

these mothers go off to work each
day discussing the lives of their
children who depend on their petty
wage. toddlers that were not taken
from them when they slipped across
the border are in the care of older
siblings who play a role in the latest
unwritten history of the meek. the
saints they insist are watching over
them but I think tired gods are debating
how long to care for these women in
the city where Auden and Trotsky
once lived.   thousands of miles away
people in the villages that have slipped
into memory live extravagantly poor,
pick the coffee for the rich consumed
on Wall Street and weep arguing with
God in the fields, at the saintly altars
and standing before colorful cathedral
paintings. each Saturday you will find
the mothers in the local Catholic church
wiping dust from the Virgen de Guadalupe,
sweeping the church floor and in a low
voice talking about the cruelties that
keep them turning restlessly at night
in the apartments. sometimes, they sit
on the stoop with the kids staring at the
white tour vans with passengers snaping
pictures of the birthplace of Hip Hop,
shrugging their shoulders at the Brown kids
and convinced everyone on the stoop is illegal
for this shitty we the people world that never
hears the barrio scream.

THE BAKERY

after the service, I walked
down second avenue to a
spot beside the newspaper
shop now so out of fashion
for electronic times with an
old man sitting inside slung
over printed news. Sunday.
I was on my way to Moishe's
to pick up Kosher pastries
from a grandmotherly baker
who sometimes shared with
me her memories of the murder
of European Jews. I trembled
listening to her stories, a Puerto
Rican and Jewish widow, two
souls exiled in Babylon, looking
for lost Eden and living in a country
crueler from day to day. I thought
about the young Guatemalan couple
sheltered in my apartment, speaking
of atrocities done in the name of the
a government supported by Uncle
Sam. I never doubted that despite not
having crossed into the promised land
Moishe's pastry would put a smile on
their faces. I knew the young couple
like the baker who always called me
darling lived with voids prayer could
not fill. Vast darkness. I thought now
would be a good time for God to appear
and come clean.

WOKE FLESH

we have words for the world of lies
that have made dark-skinned bodies
bleed since the first dishonest years
when preachers said Indians have
nearly disappeared like their white
God desired for their brazen grand
theft. we have words for the world
of lies that for centuries enslaved
Black bodies with the evil that still
suffocates life out of them at traffic
stops, in a squad car, an innocent run
down public streets, in police jails,
on children's playgrounds or when
hands are raised in the air. we have
words for the lies that try to cover
up the truth about a young unarmed
Brown boy who was riddled with police
bullets in an alley, why an innocent Latino
man was suffocated in a park by evil
done to him by cops and why a gay
Latina teen was shot by badged men
in Denver. we who dare to speak protest
the ignorance, the violence and shameless
racist justification of wrong. we who dare
to march will not walk lightly on the
killing streets, fear your riot squads,
take the blame for all things the filthy
rich have done to the fuming white
middle-class and working-class poor
or stop being your dark-faced impossible
to deflect justice demanding sidewalk
menace.

DREAM

dream like you found
lost Eden with a wide
open door. never look
back to the barren earth
you crossed that holds
the ashes of those you
love. never forget life
finds ways to holler march
on. dream with your arms
stretched wide enough to
hug our big old earth.

UNMENTIONABLE

in the news, the classrooms,
university bookstores and
places of intelligent deliberation
America leaves us entirely out
of the conversation.

I have tried walking invisibly
in the dying cities, muted by teachers
in schools, even praying out loud
in churches to fill thoughts with
Brown lives.

I have moved in America with a
mixed race life, wondered about
her desire not to know people like
me and speculated about the eyes
looking at me.

I have to ask what do you see when
looking: my Blackness, Indianness, a
Spanish world of sin, a slurred mixed
race human being? Perhaps, the fate
of invisibility!

REAR WINDOW

some questions are raised just
looking out of a tenement window
listening to the kids on the block
choosing up a game of stickball.
they come with the same Spanglish
words that invent us and shout inside
our heads loud enough for others not
to hear. we go to these questions first
with every broken English word looking
for clues about how to live in the next
hour of a new day that will hardly let
us breathe. one day you begin to ask
the name of the only red-headed girl
who never finished ninth grade and
died of a drug overdose on the roof
of her boyfriend's building. will she
make it to the loving arms of God the
preachers speak? what will she do for
eternity? will she enjoy the company
of Angels and have long conversations
in a flowered garden with la Virgen de
Guadalupe? some questions show up
at the window five minutes late like they
have the right to interrupt, they look like
the earth in the little park surrounding the
roots of trees and they beg to be noticed
above the street noise.

TEN COMMANDMENTS

I thought reading the Bible was
a simple thing and no different
from going to a Cecil B. DeMille
epic movie portraying scriptural
narrative to entertain the public
and attract inner-city kids with
technicolor delights. I remember
sitting on a stoop with friends
talking about the film The Ten
Commandments thinking the
white actor, Charlton Heston,
who was impersonating Moses
definitely did not know a damn
thing about being set adrift on
the Nile in a reed basket to flee
state-sponsored racial murder.
shit, we all looked at Angel who
happened to be on the stoop
because his father survived the
slaughter of innocents, floated
in the dark across the Rio Grande,
walked across Texas and made
it to the Bronx. nonetheless, we
loved the movie directed by the
Episcopalian who was half-Jewish
and later in life we confessed reading
scripture is nothing like enjoying a
Hollywood religious epic. when I
got to seminary the master of the
Hebrew Bible that taught me how
to read interpretively was Phyllis
Trible and she introduced me to
the method of rhetorical criticism
that scared me nearly to death.
I learned a new way to read and

made lots of interpretive mistakes
Trible graciously corrected. yet,
I wonder about looking at the
Bible stories without accounting
for cultural context. before the
flood waters come let me say
those old movies with preacher
peculiarities and Trible's exegesis
instruction to understand Holy words
sure let me appreciate Moses who
was "slow of speech, and of a slow
tongue" (Exod. 4:10) but I know for
a fact he was unlike the white man
who went from Moses on the silver
screen to president of the protect our
guns, NRA.

LADY

she knew all the streets in the
neighborhood and the lingering
dreams woven into the lives of
the people who lived on them.
I imagined in sleep she relived
good days on the beach in Puerto
Rico, the taste of the ocean in
the air, laughter getting louder
and louder with the aging day,
the faint scent of criollo chicken
floating out of hampers filled with
all kinds of food and swimming with
friends to float just above forbidden
depths. her image still strolls the
sands of Orchard Beach that called
her out on Bronx summer weekends
where she made it a practice to take
time slowly with what she managed
to shape into a life. I did not ever
know her very well, only spent ten
years of life under her roof and the
sound of her broken English voice
burns in a past whose music I confess
to have forgotten. But, you should
hear on the nights I sit beneath the
stars to weep with Angels that I call
this woman by the name that lets
me remember her face, mother!

THE AMERICAS

the governor of a state
named after the Sioux first

nation sent a message to
inhumanely jailed migrants

saying call me when you're
an American. on this side

of the Atlantic there are
other Americas scorched

by her country the violent,
this northern land to which

women and children flee to
find sanctuary, this place that

calls youth who have broken
hearts that begged abuelas

to let them go, this nation where
runaways learned to read the

wind and trust the stolen earth
given a name Christ himself

does not know. listen, you don't
need a crystal ball to determine

the United States is not alone
America and if the good governor

and her spell-bound crowd take
a moment they will learn that in

this part of the world, long before
the depiction of expulsion from

Eden was painted on the ceiling
of the Sistine Chapel, Nero burned

Rome or Christ set foot in Europe
the people seeking asylum were

here and every place from Canada,
Central America and the Cape Horn

are dearest and oblivious citizens
America!

TWIN TOWERS

I remember the day jets
crashed into the twin towers
about a mile from my first
pastoral charge. my tongue
fumbled for God's word at
the sight of the wickedness
unfolding. I wondered about
the fate of friends who worked
in the building, the death of the
innocent from the Americas and
across the globe, the spirituality
of terror that left its mark and
the fear of the coming piety of
revenge. I have not stopped
talking to the dead, the friends
who perished, strangers gone
whose names freshen my love
and the terror given a place by
those disfiguring divine words.
sometimes, I dream sentences
to speak to the dead and those
with hearts broken by grief but
they are imperfect and even the
scriptures beg me to keep silent
in the name of the dead carried

always on the tip of the world's

own tongue.

SITTING

I have a good hand of cards
to play though nature in me

is not what it was some forty
years ago. I ask sometimes in

prayer to witness the perfect
days of children laughing, the

sound of the ocean beating on
the banks of Spanish speaking

beaches, long walks with my
kids down wooded paths until

the evening drifts in and to know
the joy of more Augusts to observe

the flight of monarch butterflies
on their way to the Sierra Mountains

in Mexico where they will arrive
in time to color the forest for the

Day of the Dead. I look forward
to more days not to forget, seeing

the truth of justice discouraging
the absence of peace and finally

to find myself old enough to laugh
irrepressibly at the idea that God

is a bearded old white guy dressed
in sandals and a robe.

GOOD SAMARITAN

tell me who was the nameless
man left on the side of the road
for dead by a priest and idol worship
slayer from the days of Moses? what
ritual impurity did they want to avoid
with their evading cultural habits? tell
me what was the name of the victim
of robbers that even Angels refused
company and whose voice grew hoarse
pleading for aid? when I sit in the filthy
park on the Lower East Side it occurs to
me that religion is more than rules to follow,
formal institutions and the morally revolting
idea love for a suffering human being results
in permanent infection that requires God's
punishment. I prefer to think those left on the
road to die in pits of utter terror deserve far
more than the world of exclusive belief that
does not weep for victims. Let me assure you
the religiously heretical and allegedly racially
inferior Samaritan in that old Bible story reminds
me of Carmen from Southern Boulevard who
said we must love those God places in the way
or as Auden once put it step aside and die. damn,
I look up and down the streets and feel it necessary
to say those who suffer are entirely mine!

PALESTINE

thousands of miles away
the bombs ending the lives
of Palestinian children do
not break a single chain to
say the hungry, the violated
and the Palestinians are human
beings. how easily we forget
the names of the boys shot for
taunting soldiers in the occupied
land, how sad that people once
delivered the land of milk and
honey see no reason for the
vulnerable to claim their right
to stolen land. will we ever hear
the stones speak in the hands
of Gaza's children who throw
them? when will the country of
my citizenship that inflicts the
wounds and pays for lies beat
swords into ploughshares and
say not a penny more until the
complicated talks begin to deliver
darkness to light? time to think
of the men, women and children
that have lost their right to speak
far away from an America that
does not think of them and too
quickly equates Israel with prophetic
Judaism and looks away when that
privileged State ignores the God
who opposes its militarism and
favors the weak.

THE WAIT

I placed my head on the desk
below the print of Oscar Romero
shot at the altar while consecrating
the body of Christ. I looked at it
a few times remembering how he
carried the death of Jesus each day
in his ministry for the sake of the
life of the poor promised to them by
a crucified God. I was startled by the
phone numerous times hoping that was
the call that you safely crossed the border
and were closing the hundreds of miles
from this eastern city quickly for the first
time in a very different life. I did not need
a single word of confirmation from a red
letter New Testament to convince me that
a divine plan was upon your flight, Christ
died for it long ago, and so Romero, the
Jesuits, Elba, Selena, Rufina, Ramiro, Silvia
and tens of thousands more in a past too near
that keeps threatening to consume our hearts.
the call finally came, you crossed the river
without a single sighting of the servants of a
vengeful God. kind Brown people placed
you on a flight and I waited grateful at the
other end reading the final hours like they
were ancient scrolls describing the meaning
of life.

NECA

sister, in six decades including nearly
two of them lost you received no more
than one letter from me. we did stop
talking to each other when children for
reasons entirely beyond our years and
began whispering beyond the silences
in young adult life. I am glad you have
realized some of your dreams and faced
the indifference the Spanglish hating era
has sent your way. I never stopped thinking
about the long walks to public school, the
visits to the Zoo, the wandering in city parks
and the annual Easter Mass in the basement
of the Catholic church with a sorrowing crowd
of non-English speakers. sister, I see you never
forgot to listen to the songbirds that visit your
window, hear the laughter of children who still
skip rope on the block or pay attention to the
islands of Puerto Rican girls on the sidewalk
sharing gossip. I am glad you carried the light
that keeps the world's eyes wide open for us.
sister, when life was made of sadness you refused
to cry, when we faced the hungry table in the
kitchen you smiled and never once forgot to
find goodness rolling across the face of the
block though in tears. sister, I give God thanks
for your belief in people, kindness and what is
beautiful in life.

LET US DREAM

I walked down a Lower East Side
Alphabet street looking for missing
pieces of sanity in the alleys, on the
corners and the Perez grocery store.
an old woman with a red scarf hugging
her shoulders told me it was for sale
but her marvelous memory loss could
not tell me who was peddling it for the
barrio. I wanted to find them but it was
like chasing a leaf of newspaper blown
by the wind and floating up until entirely
unseen.   words rushed into my head
from the melancholic old-world ballads
that washed over me from my mother's
vinyl spinner that is now no more than
a museum piece and I felt a longing for
the gentle touch of heaven, love and the
deep sense of wanting America not to
exist without us.

GOLGOTHA

I bet you didn't know we walked

across the desert saying prayers

that are hundreds of years old in

Spanish. each one of us carried a

piece of the mystery you look for

in your segregated hour that finds

a way to keep us absent on land that

called us home. we were raised across

the border you see reading the Holy

Book with stories of the losers in the

world who talked to God and Angels with

ruffled feathers. I bet you didn't know

we learned to sit between light and shade

on the way to aging cities and nourished

ourselves with spiked cactus on warm

sand. we have not lived comfortably for

more weeks than can be recalled and no

one among us believes in mirages though

after stumbling across the border our days

are occupied by the theological mistake that

light is not good and God in your penal colony

in love with tribalism, ignorance and racial

hate only speaks English.

IMAGINARY LAND

you want to leap into the
world you heard about
from an Irish-American
priest who fetched it out
of the dark from a map of
gracious dreams. you
imagine the gods in it
apologizing and saying
they will make up the
lost time and sweep away
any fears. you taste wine
and bread like new in your
scabbed years, experience
the imaginary land seep into
your marrow and from the
places that do not cry pray
to wake up in the place named
by the priest!

HEAVEN IS A CAFÉ

I went to the Ukrainian café on
Avenue A to be with the people
pouring their wounds into each
others' cups. a waitress listened
at the counter to a story with tears
in her eyes. there wasn't a soul in
the place untroubled by darkened
days or the candles bought in the
botanica not lighting a way. the
place was busy with chatter yet
everyone was equally unable to
say what they aimed to find to
shed the unbearable weight of
sadness. it occurred to me then
the Argentian poet Borges imagined
heaven to be a great library but I
thought maybe it's no more than
a café where a few feet to the left
or right people employ different
languages at their tables hoping to
unravel the mysteries philosophers
and theologians with fancy words
carefully and thoroughly blur.

THE FOURTH WORLD

I have waited for the clouds
to one day spell your name, to
hear the people who start each
day clean in the condominiums
say it right, to find it written in
the pages of the required books
of schools, college history classes,
seminaries of divine learning or
mysteriously written on parched
earth to be seen from heaven. I have
waited for you not to fall like Alice
in the rabbit hole, to become visible
like you are for the martyred men
and women that sob for the unseen
in the world. I have waited for them to
understand original people like you
belong to the beginning of this patch
of ground and this city ignorant about
world's neither Black nor White. I have
waited for the intellectuals, philosophers,
theologians, governors, pastors, priests
and activists to confess this land was
home to you long before time learned
to speak in English and expensive words
divided the world.

NAKED

the words

are wet again

in this late Spring

reminding us of those

that have gone

before.

the talk

pours from

public mouths a

little less confused

now

that life is more

open.

each day

sees the country

grow with

darker

human beings

confirming

Whitman's poetic

vision.

people with

red caps still

running around

with guns, knives,

gallows and white

screams yet disbelieve

America cannot stand

their

     rotten

        thoughts.

CHILD

nothing has changed for
us, the Spanish we speak,
calloused hands, breaking
backs and incensed eyes
know it. we hear it on the
nightly news seeing white
faces scream, in the shops
where they say in unwritten
ways go back to your country
and in the schools that refuse
to teach Brown human beings
belong. nothing has changed
though signs no longer read
we serve whites only no Spanish
or Mexicans. nothing has changed
and wherever we go is just another
colored waiting room on the way
to a grave. nothing has changed and
this leaves us more than half past
the sixties shaking our heads and
applauding every broken English
child citizen with raised fists.

THE GARDEN

last night sitting beneath
a last quarter moon, the
statue of Saint Anthony in
in the garden, the traffic of
cars passing like chariots
the fence, I leaned into the
figure full of promise and
felt the world for a moment
steered toward kindness. I
sat in the lifting wind in foolish
prayer reciting love from the
Paduan Saint's hands could be
in ours. I thought about coming
morning and the news from the
world to be printed and shared
on screens, the transfer of each
others stories held in breakfast
hands, places across the earth
with woe and it was impossible
not to conclude God will interrupt
the devil's waltz, soon.

PROGNOSIS

the year of illness has taught

every one to mourn, how to wail

in the hospital, say farewell to

those held dear and heal the

sorrowing heart. we are all in

this heartbreaking season the

inexperienced grievers living in

a world drowning in tears. we

now know the Angel of death by

name, heard his fatal singing in

the languages of the earth, hid our

faces from this messenger with

masks and searched in this time

of what next for comfort against

the virus undoing us. today, we

wait nonetheless for the flowers

to open, love to take hold of us

in the dark and the jubilant gravity

of life again ours.

STOP ASIAN HATE

your elderly mother came to find
new life in a world discovered on
maps that never seemed to run fast
enough for freedom. she has lately
disappeared from the daily visits to
the Asian market, afternoon walks,
visits with friends on a favorite park
bench and you tell me she weeps at
the sight of little girls holding up signs
saying stop Asian hate. she is tired of
hearing the news about elderly Asian
women beaten in public, others who
are dead due to hate and feeling like
her skin, eyes and name justify lies
about who is to blame for declining
public health. I will walk with you
on the stony road, swim with you in
troubled waters and speak out beside
you against the lies, the bigotry and the
people who know nothing about bowing
their heads.

THE EDGE

the laughter is returning each
night with vigor, faces smile
in everyday life for the eye to
see and the lost conversations
are catching up with this new
public moment. the clouds have
names painted on them in the
colors of the rainbow, young
mothers stroll with infants on
the streets, girls named Maria
and boys called Jose are at play
in the warming days of June. I
walk pass a sidewalk table of a
fashionable café and overhear a
group of friends in conversation
and wishing to know from each
other the history of the last hard
year. amused by the thought one
among them says the ground is
still beneath us and the assassin
sickness will continue to slowly
tumble into the abyss. shall I call
this thought prayer? the friends
chuckle and order another round
of drinks!

ENDLESS

in the city where the factories
were closed, the smell of Puerto
Rican cooking is occasionally in
the air, no Cathedral is found, the
jobless pray in their apartments,
wear crosses and eat rice with a
side of marmalade bread. the old
women spend their time chatting
on the stoop, blessing tired faces
and blowing kisses to the children
with eyes folded to sadness who find
many ways to play. on this block,
the smiles, flowers on fire escapes,
salsa floating out of windows, dreams
trapped in the tenements are signs from
heaven speaking the Spanglish of an
inexhaustible God. here we understand
each other's words, call out the anatomy
of sorrow, invite the meaning of happiness,
carry memories from distant lands and find
the company of love.

AOC

that Puerto Rican woman
elected to Congress with
her razor-sharp brilliance,
love for justice and gift for
riding storms knows life on
these shores will never be
silenced by the blind hatred
of white supremacist fools
who just love to push equality,
justice and freedom apart in
the name of ruin and wicked
lynch craving souls.

JUDGED

We will be judged for withholding a welcome to strangers and love for people fleeing destitution, hunger and violence.

We will be judged for attempting to live the good life specified in the creeds, while turning away from the God who liberates slaves, enters the world undocumented, becomes flesh in a human being from the despised side of town and is crucified on the other side of a border.

We will be judged for accommodating a white supremacist religion that pines for an abominable past, for not objecting to a foreign policy of terror for Central American nations and for silencing the voices of widows and orphans with dark faces.

We will be judged for the ignorance of elected officials, the fettered intelligence of citizens, the exclusive equality of democracy and for denying the power of love to break all barriers.

We will be judged for saying little to nothing at all to a Vice President who choose in Guatemala not to be a voice for the voiceless, who gagged Emma Lazarus, and neglected to confess the US paid for a genocidal war against indigenous humanity in Guatemala and the Salvadoran poor.

We will be judged by a Crucified God, the truth about Central American people skinned alive, set on fire, and raped to death by soldiers Uncle Sam trained in Georgia.

We will be judged by the screams of victims from the Northern Triangle, consenting to an imperial White House with a human face and forgetting God takes sides.

THE BLOCK

walking the block with a small
silvery moon lighting the way, I
hear the sound of shouting voices
coming from open windows, phones
on the stoop ringing Latin beats, the
national anthem blaring from a
television set with an audience
waiting for the baseball game, the
cops on the corner beating the shit
out of hollering Bosco for the crime
of being Black. the unemployed old
men are up early to play dominoes, the
junkies are prowling the streets to
gather money for a fix, winos are
on Simpson Street passing around
a bottle of wine in a brown paper
sack, and abuelas who fix everything
are on their way to the local A&P
to pick up food. today, there isn't a
corner that doesn't remind us Jesus
was born to a teen mother, unemployed,
homeless, hungry, brutally arrested,
racially despised and hung on a tree
from which he called to heaven without
a single word of English.

MOTHER AND CHILD

she loved him, dressed him,
feed him each morning before
school, listened to him in the
kitchen barely able to sit in a
chair telling stories about Art
class and laughed when her
boy smiled each time she tried
to speak a little English. sometimes,
in the evening they would watch
a television show that made them
laugh too loud and think it would
never be so good as that instant,
never more home than that ground
floor apartment and never more
gentle than the gracious love shared
that dissolved fear and even the dread
of not having papers. the mother could
not stop the boy from growing and
growing any more than raising her hands
could stop drifting clouds. more than
once, he was beaten up on the block by
the Turban Taps gang and white 41st
Precinct cops. one day the boy came
home from school carrying a single
sweet-smelling blush colored rose,

kissed her on the cheek, and announced
the good news that Princeton University
had given him a place in their art program.
she felt the mountaintop entered the apartment
and they laughed too loud, again. she looked
at her son saying in her insulted tongue, ¡Ave
Maria Purísima, que buenas noticias!

BILLY ABRAHAM

he touched the lives of
students these many years,
wrote with decisive genius
and left his beloved church
some of the greatest thoughts
on faith in the English language.
this Irish child of heaven offered
prayers in many places about the
dusty elements from God, the cravings
in the human soul and people destined
to be more than heaps of dust. he
spent time dreaming of lightness in
the dark, listened to quivering hearts
in Sunday school classes and noticed
the world of strife in them begging
for release. he made it easier to live
in the world so unexpectedly departed
like a leaf removed from the branch of
an Autumn tree before winter. dear colleague,
friend and child of God your departure
sweeps across noisy spaces and I must
say the weeping is for you a monument
placed in the halls, classrooms and churches
you lived.

www.ingramcontent.com/pod-product-compliance
Lightning Source LLC
Chambersburg PA
CBHW060348090426
42734CB00011B/2078